Black Lawyer Confidential: Keys to Success

Johnnie L. Finch, Jr., Esq.

Black Lawyer Confidential: Keys to Success

Copyright © 2018 by Post Script Publishing

ISBN 978-0-578-20637-0

To my loving wife, Meron, and my children, Johnnie III "John John" and Yohanna. Also, to my wonderful mother and father, Thelma and John Finch, Sr. And I could never forget about my very good friends, Jermaine, Des, Jerriel, Kevin, Terrence, Colbert, Torrence, DJ, and Marshall.

I would like to give a special thanks to Ashley Mitchell and Michelle Thomas, Ph.D. for providing their insight in preparation of publishing this book. Also, a big thank you to Tim Bowser for always being there whenever needed. Your hard work and great attention to detail is certainly appreciated!

Acknowledgements

With God, all things are possible. I thank you for leading and guiding me in my journey.

Table of Contents

Letter to the Reader
(Potential Law Student/Future Lawyer)

As I sit in my favorite coffee shop contemplating the purpose of this book, I think to myself, "I've practiced law for exactly five years". However, it feels as if it has been more like 10-15 years. I can recall the times I had before practicing law. I lived a normal life. I worked my one and a half jobs, hung out with friends, went on the occasional date, enjoyed church, read books, vacationed, and paid bills. It was all so simple. Law school consisted of me studying, a lot of alone time, and eventually preparing for the bar. It's exhausting at its best! Becoming an attorney is an appointment that overtakes your entire being. Your mind challenges you to wonder, "Was I made for this? Can I adhere to its rigid norms"? The challenge, should you choose to accept it, is a constant test of moral, ethical, spiritual, financial, and emotional dynamics. There will be many days when you ask yourself, "What am I doing? Is all of this work really worth it? What happened to my social life? Do I have what it takes? Am I going to be a successful lawyer or just end up in debt, repaying my tuition and student loans?" There will be days when you'll want to flee the profession but there's also something about this choice of work that is highly addictive. Everyone likes the feeling of winning. Especially, when winning means that you were able to outwit your opponent. However, it is more fulfilling to effectuate positive change.

What's the purpose of this book? If you are considering becoming a lawyer, this book will give you firsthand insight into the unspoken challenges of the profession. If you are an African-American or a minority, then my hope is that this book will help you understand the culture that exists within the legal system, which is not commonly taught during legal education. Common themes will rear their ugly heads from the very first day of law school, up until you retire, or maybe even die. It is my prayer and desire that many will see this book as a *confirmation of their choice to enter the profession*, however, it is also my hope to paint a realistic picture of how law practice feels, tastes, and smells.

Quotes from some of my friends who happen to be top lawyers and are under the age of 40, will be provided throughout this book. These quotes should give you insight, motivation, or advice regarding attending law school and becoming a lawyer.

Relevant Question:

Why should you read this book before attending law school? First, law school is monetarily expensive and extremely time consuming. Secondly, it's not a practice where many can simply coast along a straight and narrow path to success, especially, as an ethnic minority. The reality is: no one skips through the tulips in this arena. In fact, your livelihood is contingent upon hard work and perseverance. I'm sure it might be easier to dabble in other areas and become distracted with a social life, but you must push extremely hard!

In preparation for this reading, I've studied the stories of greats, such as, Thurgood Marshall, who fought with the National Association for the Advancement of Colored People in the thick of the Civil Rights Movement, and later, Johnnie Cochran, who in the early 1990's, battled a more systematic racism with the Los Angeles Police Department and other government principalities. To keep an even playing field, I've also interviewed many of my peers, whom are both Black and White, old and young, to add value to my perspective.

If my experience is unique, I'll be sure to cue the reader in on these specific thoughts of my own. Basically, I'll make you aware whenever I'm sharing a super personal experience. Furthermore, I am a follower of Christ, which will be exhibited throughout this book. This book encompasses all of which my experiences have shown me. I'm writing from my personal spiritual position, however, no one should feel alienated. I've saved my politically correct life for the courtroom (later, we will dive heavily into the "PC Life"). As a Black lawyer, you realize that being a lawyer is a profession and there exists a line in the sand that you better not cross. It will feel like war for anyone becoming a lawyer, however, for an ethnic minority, you're going to feel as if you are fighting two wars. In this book, I aim to outline the playing field or at least make that battleground a little more visible for the reader.

In an effort to enlighten the reader more about myself as an individual, and my experience in the legal profession, I will provide a brief list of stats regarding myself:

- Elizabeth City State University, BA Criminal Justice, BS Sociology
- Regent University School of Law, JD
- Criminal Defense Attorney (I've handled quite a few matters from human trafficking to police brutality)
- Civil Rights (brief impactful experience)
- Plaintiff's Attorney (I've made some good money for my clients)
- Ph.D. - Self-Appointed Honorary in Balancing Conflict Between the System, African-Americans and the Poor (You can't buy one of these).

The Bottom Line:

Black lawyers must engage in one hell of a fight in order to succeed. You're either all in 300% or you're barely eating, and depressed, or both. From the day you pass the bar, consider your life as if you're metaphorically jumping into the deep end of an ocean while not wearing a life jacket.

Mentions:

Right off the top, Mitch Jackson, my good friend and mentor, Alicyia Klinchloe, Nicole Abboud, Kyle Jones, and Cliff Smith, have proven to be super valuable relationships. I'd give my right foot for these types of friends and mentors; which you'll need to survive. Going back to law school, Matt "Ammo" Morris, Andrew Rice and tall Matt Morris gave me my first lesson that enabled me to grasp the big picture regarding the leverage game. My brothers, Greg, John, and Daryl kept me leveled, and John Bachelor held me down. One professor, Stephen Pfiefer, was kind enough to give me respect and told me that I had special gifts that could change the game, whereas, most professors would stare as if I didn't belong. They were extra helpful academically, however, provided no extra words of confirmation or encouragement. Others professors, such as Scott Pryor, James Duane, Lynn Marie Kohm, and Dean Natt Gantt, all played a tremendous role in molding my educational journey.

We will speak more regarding this topic later, however, just know that your circle is EVERYTHING! Your circle is your "lawyer currency". You don't get very far in law practice without help. Your NETWORK will always take you where the WORK cannot.

"Ask God for wisdom every morning."
~ *(NLT Bible, II Chronicles 2:10)*

Current America

Donald Trump is now the Commander-In-Chief and POTUS. Police-Black relationships are boiling over with the effect of camera phones, and I would choose as a primary practice, Criminal Defense. My career places me directly in the middle of everything. I like to refer to myself as a "street lawyer". I'm with the people every day. My definition of a street lawyer is the "anti-corporate lawyer", where it's never business as usual. I'm a lawyer to the common man, whose primary focus is grassroots in the community. I am a lawyer who identifies with the poor and disrespected, who brings justice to the poor, who educates the poor about law, who realizes that he may be his client's last and only voice for their life, a lawyer who connects the needs of the community to the upper class and powers that be; judges and legislators. Moreover, I'm a lawyer whose duty is to mentor and groom the next generation of street lawyers and teach them the importance of the "street lawyer" focus. I'm a lawyer who can be trusted and one who treats his clients as if they were his own children.

Being an African-American male myself, gives me the necessary insight and innate knowledge of the hardships and mitigating circumstances that may arise and causes defendants to have contact with the police and the criminal justice system in the first place. This also has major advantages when it comes to being a "street lawyer" because there's practically little to no degrees of separation between my clients and I. Keep in mind that I practice law in my hometown. Therefore, we grew up in the same neighborhoods, played basketball together, had crushes on the same girls as youngsters, etc. The only difference is that I went to law school and was blessed with a strong father who took the time to explain life to me. However, I know their language, when they're telling the truth, and when they're feeling embarrassed or unsure.

A good lawyer understands his client's interests, so when a client tells me that he would rather go to jail than be placed on probation, or go to prison rather than snitch, I don't have to wonder regarding the reasoning behind their sentiments. I completely understand their reasoning. Making key decisions while under pressure is so much easier to execute during plea negotiations or trial when I thoroughly understand my client's point of view.

First Level of Training: Law School – What Can Minorities Expect?

This section has little to do with race but everything to do with painting a mental picture of situations one may experience when entering law school. This section will discuss *my* personal experience, which may differ from others.

I had zero thoughts on what to expect when entering into law school. I felt confident because of my previous experience with formal education. I knew that I wasn't dumb, but I wasn't sure how I would measure up when competing with the best of the best. Most of my confidence was derived from my spiritual mindset. I felt as if there were no way that I could fail because this was my path.

"Everyone has a plan until they get hit in the mouth."
~ Mike Tyson

Well, the 1L class, Legal Research and Writing, hit me directly in the mouth, over and over and over again! I remember looking at classmates and feeling extremely inadequate. My fellow students were so well polished and prepared. Quickly, I realized that I could not make up for the preparation gap. My peers would only get better and better as I struggled to figure things out. And once I did figure things out, my poor grades would average with the good grades I'd later obtain, but would never measure up, comparably.

At that point, I stopped looking at everyone else and started working on myself. Frankly, I simply stopped caring about what everyone else was thinking and doing. The thirty minutes that I would normally allocate towards preparing my outfit for the day turned into 5-7 minutes, and my social media daily exercise turned into Contract and Property prep audios and outlines. On Friday nights, I was at the library instead of the bar. Coincidentally, so were the top students in our class.

Light bulb!

Remember...

"Everyone is a beast until they get dropped into the jungle."
~ Dr. Eric Thomas

Bottom Line:

Compete with yourself but use others as raw motivation.

_____

The Playing Field

I'm not a stats guy, however, unless you attend a historically Black law school, you'll probably be in a school which is at most, 10% Black. You'll be in classes of about 80 students and maybe 2 or 3 students will be African-American. This is where your education really begins. Personally, I'm from a small town in North Carolina, where the population is about 50/50 Black to White. I chose Regent University, founded by Pat Robertson, in Virginia Beach for law school. The environment at Regent was very safe and serene. During preview weekend, I was sold when I learned that we had mandatory 15-minute devotions before every class, and the curriculum focused upon grooming lawyers not to separate their spiritual beliefs from their practice.

The experience was great for me because I attended Elizabeth City State University for undergrad where virtually everyone was Black. Let's call this "educational cross-training". I was in a totally new world at Regent. I believe God is always equipping us for the long game. Before law school, I worked for the State of North Carolina as a Juvenile Justice Officer in a detention center. I had no aspirations of law school at the time, but dealing with those young brothers from broken homes was an invaluable experience. Just in case you're wondering about my decision to attend law school, I call it divine intervention, regarding the way it all came together. Even during my non-focused years when I wasn't taking advantage of the moment nor my God-given talent and was idling through life after undergrad, the blueprint was being laid.

"For I know the plans I have for you", declares the
LORD, plans to prosper you and not to harm you,
plans to give you hope and a future."
~ (NIV Bible, Jeremiah 29:11)

Resourceful Reading Tools to Consider

These books will help you manage and assess
relationships, as well as, focus your thinking:

"Never Eat Alone" by Keith Ferrazi

"Business Secrets from the Bible" by Rabbi Lapin

"1 Minute Businessman's Devotional" by Mike
Murdock

"Speak Like Churchill, Stand Like Lincoln" by James
Humes

"Lawyer's Life" by Johnnie Cochran

"48 Laws of Power" by Robert Greene

"The Tipping Point" by Malcolm Gladwell

"David and Goliath" by Malcolm Gladwell

"Devil in the Grove: Thurgood Marshall, the
Groveland Boys, and the Dawn of a New America"
by Gilbert King

"How to Win Friends and Influence People" by Dale
Carnegie

"Frederick Douglas: The Story of an American
Slave" by Frederick Douglas

"The Lawyer Marketing Formula" by David Ward

Selecting a Law School to Attend

It's completely natural to feel anxious, nervous and even afraid when trying to select which law school to apply to or attend. I will be providing you with a candid look at law school and law practice through the lense of an African American with no law experience at all, whatsoever. I've learned the hard way, so take what you can from my journey.

Tiers

If you can get accepted into a top tier law school, then by all means, attend that school. It will enhance your network of potential employers, your profile, and assist you with gaining access to excellent internships, pretty much of your choice. Many employers won't consider your application if you didn't attend a top tier school.

If you want to be a general practitioner, top tier schools are NOT essential. You may want to consider attending the school in your state that has the best legal network to connect to. On the other hand, there's no need to go to Yale if you know that you want to practice Family Law in your hometown. Attend a law school that is close to home and intern with a local attorney.

Caveat

If you already know that you want to practice law within your local community or already have a job lined up, a top tier school is not as important. If this were your situation, you would want to attend the law school that is located closest to your future place of employment so that you may be available to them as an intern.

At the end of the day, more importantly, go to someone's law school somewhere! Get the best out of wherever you go and keep the aforementioned tips in mind while deciding whether or not your potential law school is ideal. If you happen to receive a low score on the LSAT (law school admissions test) and have to attend a school not of your choice or it isn't aligned with your future goals, you can always transfer to another school after your first year.

All things being equal, attend the law school that offers you the best scholarship. Keep in mind that a 3.0 G.P.A. in law school is more like a 3.8 G.P.A. in undergrad. In the history of my law school, there has been only *one* student that graduated with a 4.0 G.P.A. Therefore, make sure that you are aware of the requirements of maintaining your scholarship.

My Classmates and Perhaps Yours

Let's talk about this 10% of Black law students. Initially, I was looking for African-American peers to connect with, hold hands, and take this journey head-on, together. This was the place where I learned (silly and culturally ignorant of me) that all Blacks don't think the same. I was looking forward to latching onto the black community of law students; however, there were 3-5% that wanted nothing to do with the black law student community or me. At first glance, there appeared to be some sort of theoretical self-hate on their behalf. But looking back, THEY SIMPLY DID NOT SEE THE BENEFIT. The bottom line appeared to be that many of my Black peers had developed survival techniques that involved assimilating into the status quo, and law school was not an environment to rock the boat. Most will choose to play with the team that appears to be winning.

This leaves you with about 7% and if you're at a lower tier law school, another 2-3% more than likely won't be academically strong or focused enough to make it past the first year. Thank God, I went to law school with my longtime friend Greg, who was from the same background as myself. It's safe to say you'll probably have one or two Black students that you'll be able to see eye-to-eye with, but you probably won't be in the same class or section.

Again, this is not a book about academics. As for academics, I will say, go to law school and get with a study group that's in the "know". Get the outlines and find study partners that will help you pass. My experience is that the Black upper classmen will help. However, law school has an innate class system that does not include befriending lower classmen. They feel that 1L students must "earn the keep" before they deserve any respect from the upper classmen.

"Be yourself. Don't get caught up in the politics of it all and play it cool. Don't let them see you sweat!"
~ J. Gonzalez, Esq.

Study Groups and Learning Styles

I've asked Ashley Mitchell, an African American 2L student at North Carolina Central University, for her opinion regarding study groups and she has provided us with this extremely helpful insight:

"Study groups work great for some and terrible for others. There are several advantages to taking part in study groups. One advantage of being a part of a study group is the idea that those who are stronger in a particular subject can assist those who are weaker in that subject. This allows the "stronger" individual to review the material while allowing the "weaker" individual to learn and understand the material; it's a win-win situation! In addition, being able to just talk through multiples and essay questions with your peers can sometimes open your eyes to solutions or issues that you were unaware of.

Though study groups have several advantages, there are some disadvantages to study groups, as well. Often times, we choose the members of our study groups by selecting people who are our friends or people who have similar ideas and beliefs. This can be problematic

21

because being in a study group with friends can lead to the endless gossiping, laughter, or anything other than studying. Also, being in a study group with people who share similar or identical beliefs and ideas can be problematic because growth occurs most when we are challenged. If two individuals have the exact same ideas, they cannot challenge each other to think beyond and grow.

The key is finding the right study group for your learning style, and staying focused on the goal. Maybe your best friends shouldn't be in your study group if you feel you'll be easily distracted? Maybe studying in solitude and checking in with a group periodically is better? Whatever your style, find it and master it quickly. If you realize study groups are not good for you, study alone and keep it moving.

In addition to finding the right study group, you should also take the time to figure out what type of learning techniques work best for you. For some, simply reading notes and talking through the material works. For others, listening to audio recordings over and over again works better. Personally, writing rules out on a dry erase board endlessly until the material flows easily from my mind worked best for me."

If you are unaware of your learning style, whether verbal or audial, that is something that you will definitely need to figure out before attending law school. Tailoring your learning techniques to foster your approach to learning the course material will be absolutely vital to your success in law school.

The Academics

Here's what you can expect during the first few weeks of school. When I spoke in class, especially in Socratic method style, I personally felt as though I was being judged as a spokesman for the entire Black race. You may receive an assortment of looks, stares, glares, smiles, and smirks. Candidly, my inner feelings as I answered a question in class, was that if I answered a question incorrectly, I'd be seen as the dumb Black guy and this would serve as confirmation that we are not as academically strong as a race. If I answered the question correctly, "Who does this guy think he is? He will never be on our level". Sometimes, I'd receive a very dismissive smirk. Worst, "What is this guy doing in the same class as me?" Now that I think back, this was a peer-to-peer, personal struggle of mine. Even during a Socratic-style beating by one of my professors, I always felt like they still had my back. My assumptions and perceptions of my peers could be totally off? But remember, the way you perceive one's reaction to you may affect how you think and behave.

> *"Pay attention to details and learn from your mistakes."*
> *~ Kristin Wills, Esq.*

Many open forums took place where I heard offensive proclamations pertaining to slavery and how Black people are always complaining. These remarks were boldly exclaimed as if it were okay to be disrespectful or offensive as long as it was within an academic setting. My advice: be calm and move on. A person's ignorance is their problem, not yours. You'll need all of your energy to focus on academics. Honestly, that type of patriotism may never stop but it's preparation for the real game.

24

Those classrooms will soon be courtrooms and those staring peers will soon be judges, opposing counsel, bailiffs, law enforcement, the media, and clerks. I struggled academically during my first year of law school. My learning curve was a negative 100 and catching up was almost impossible. Mainly, I struggled because I didn't know what questions to ask, whom to ask, or what and how to study. Although I didn't turn the other cheek as I'm now suggesting you to do, those race debates didn't help me one bit on the exam. Stay focused and keep your eye on the prize.

As the semester progressed, I grew very close to some White students because even though we never spoke about it, we both hated the culture of law school and the politics behind the powers. Most of them came from working class families and were first generation law students. Honestly, I felt bitter towards some of my Black peers when I saw my White peers befriending me, while my Black peers wanted nothing to do with me. Please understand that this was my problem. Not theirs. I was spending my energy being angry about the potential lost relation. They were studying.

Life Teaching Moment:

God will always place people (despite race, creed, or color) into your life that will help elevate you to the next level. However, your eyes, and especially, mouth, must be open.

The Hierarchy

Personally, much of law school felt like a caste system where the White students and professors had an island and the Black students had a separate island within that hierarchy. I remember experiencing this while participating in intramural sports. We had some White guys in our 1L class that could really play ball. I was hoping to become a part of their team and possibly win the championship. However, there was a private meeting before the season started and all the Black guys (which ironically were not the best ballers) were somehow placed on our own team along with some decent playing White guys. What's more telling is that the gentlemen on my White peers' team were far from racist but the innate "order" was set.

New Lesson:

This was not the type of power play that I was accustomed to. Lawyer life is a thinking man's game and those guys played chess! This was the first time that I felt put in my place. But once I recognized the game, I was more equipped to play. No matter the game, always keep a watchful eye for power plays so that you can learn the game. The book, "48 Laws of Power" by Robert Greene, has many examples of this type of diplomacy. Be wise young lion.

Fast Forward to Law Practice

Once you start law practice, watch how cleverly the major players move at destroying their competition. Try your best to stay away from politics during your first 5-10 years in law practice and watch how the game is played within your locality. Each locality plays a different game and has its own distinct set of rules.

No one speaks of this hierarchy, however, everyone feels it. I was 29 years old when I started law school and had I attended law school directly after undergrad, without my experience working with the State of North Carolina, I would've been eaten alive. There's an underlying feeling that the majority won't disrupt the status quo, and during law practice, you'll notice that many lawyers are very savvy about not accepting cases that will disrupt the status quo; especially, civil rights cases.

"Focus and work hard. If you do that, you will attract the people and things around you that will make it easier to obtain your goal."
~ Daryl Hayott, Esq.

_____

Professors and Deans

Many of the law professors that you'll find in law school are academics with little to no real time lawyer experience, unless your school is new and progressive. Their personal experience may not begin to equip them with the wisdom to nurture a young minority law student. It's just how law school is designed from inception. Law schools need the highest academic professors to write papers for the law school to keep the school's ranking up to par. Despite the lack of cultural diversity, my first year law professors were bigger than life to me and I held onto their every word as law. This was one of the major advantages of learning within a Christian environment.

In regards to academic support, if your grades are not stellar, you'll be seen as, or at least I felt like I was perceived as, a failure, despite the other intangible God-given abilities you possess. However, you must trust the process. Law school can be like Wall Street. Stocks go up when higher numbers of students pass the bar exam and stocks go down when there is an increase in the number of students who fail and don't pass the bar.

"Know how to study. Stay organized."

~LeeAnne Lawrence, Esq.

My self-esteem was low when it came to my academic progress and ability to succeed as a lawyer. Then, Stephen Pfiefer walked in. During my 3rd year of law school, I took his Negotiations class. A young, successful lawyer, who worked at the most prominent firm in Virginia Beach, pulled me to the side and told me, "You've got all the tools, Johnnie Finch". Pfiefer helped me secure internships and gave excellent reference letters. I still talk with him at least once per week. So, yes, I attended law school for three years before I finally gained my first jolt of confidence and confirmation aside from my spiritual affirmations.

> *"Law school and law practice is more like a marathon than a sprint. Training and the execution of it will be forever."*
>
> ~ Derek Brown, Esq.

Law school teaches one to think like a lawyer, but it doesn't teach you how to develop your God given talent. Moot court is highly pushed upon students as the mecca of success, but that's only because a successful team can help the law school achieve merit. I don't know any lawyer who has argued moot style for the appeals court. Okay, maybe one...and they did it once. Moot court taught me to be highly formal, not too expressive, not to use my hands when speaking, and to be as dull as possible.

Consequently, it stripped me of my strengths and made me aware of my weaknesses. This was a good thing. Law school clubs are highly political and unless you're cool with the admin students who had the clout, more than likely, you'll be overlooked; outside of some super powers you possess to be the Kobe Bryant of the group or the token Black person. You'd resemble any fictional character of African-American descent that has been inconsequently inserted into the plot of a movie or TV show for the express purpose of creating an image of commercially safe, politically correct, and insipid racial harmony. You'll see this on many billboards across America.

"Try to find a mentor who knows what they're doing and is respected in the profession. You don't learn how to be a lawyer in law school and it can be tough figuring things out by yourself. Find a mentor that can show you the way and be a sound board to bounce ideas off of."
~ John Raper, Esq.

As a lawyer, you must always think for the long game. Everyone wants to be perceived as being intelligent and desire to be loved by their professors and deans; however, you must assess each mentor's influence on their own merit and ask yourself, "Does this person help me reach my ultimate goal"?

Ask yourself this ultimate goal question:

Which population do I want to serve and where are they located? What information do I need to know? Whom do I need to seek and speak with in order to reach my ultimate goal? Write your answer below.

_____
_____
_____
_____
_____
_____
_____
_____
_____
_____
_____
_____
_____
_____

Mentors

If you know that you want to become a criminal defense attorney and your Family Law professor clearly doesn't like you, it's okay. Always do your best to be cordial and continue to do your best work. But you must find an influence that propels you toward your ultimate goal. Assess quickly and make your move.

For instance, it makes more sense to connect to the dean who has roots in Illinois, where you would like to practice, than the random Property Law professor who gets a rise from embarrassing 1L's, with no litigation experience.

"Find a mentor! You think you know what you're doing, but you really didn't learn ANYTHING in law school! You need someone that is resourceful so that you can ask questions!"

~ Monique Sexton, Esq.

Leveraging Your Power

Law school life parallels law practice in so many ways. You may be an excellent lawyer, however, if you jump out of your lane too early, it can be detrimental to your career. You may be ostracized or blackballed. This goes for everyone, regardless of race, creed or color.

What was the most important lesson? The majority has the power of influence and leverage. I didn't understand this concept while I was in law school. All I knew was fight, fight, and fight. But soon, I realized that I was swinging at no one and losing a lot of energy by doing so. Eventually, I learned that there were unlimited possibilities and that I possessed limitless power, once I learned how to leverage my strengths.

Let's look at this like a war:

First, understand that the power of the law school machine is the power to control the landscape and playing field. You can't beat or maneuver around the machine because you need accreditation to sit for the bar and it would be dumb to fight it. From the moment you begin attending law school, you should find your positions of advantage and learn when and how to attack. My professors were always there to back me but I didn't know what questions to ask.

Now, there's an ensuing war and it's occurring on every scale. Success is a war. The moment you don't treat it as such, you'll find yourself treading water. Pray for discipline. As a law student, you'll get a pass for slipping or making mistakes, but in law practice, the stage and your platform is too large to give into drug addiction, chasing women, or the quick dollar.

An innate skill that I possess is making friends very quickly. The more friends I made in law school, as oppose to enemies, the easier it was to navigate the terrain and gain skills, valuable knowledge, and resources. Once you've established yourself as a force, your latter days of law school will be easier but don't let this ease weaken your armor. You'll be more likely to ruffle feathers once you've acquired more legal ammunition and machinery. Remember...the war is just beginning.

> *"Your reputation is key to your success."*
> ~ *Judge Eula Reid*

Trust Your Own Process

My first attempt at passing the bar exam was unsuccessful. Before sitting for the bar, I had three strong offers of employment lined up. It was devastating when I learned that I was unsuccessful. All of my prayers and 28-hour study sessions didn't equal a successful outcome. The first few following weeks were the worst but my support system held me down, and most of the bar members gave great words of encouragement. Most lawyers understand this process. After I pulled my head from between my legs (yes, I cried once or twice), I enrolled in a course that was provided by a prominent bar exam study tutor. A great friend of mine, Jarrette Pittman, was the bar tutor assigned to me. What did I learned? You must always be in the know.

"Be 15 minutes early for the rest of your life."
~ Willis Brantley, Esq.

I've learned invaluable information while in the bar exam study course. The secret to was passing or failing was organizing my answers, underlining subtopics, and overstating certain facts or laws in my analysis. Fast forward, the lawyer game is about deriving the relevant information and not assuming. Had I not enrolled in the course, I could've been unsuccessful 3-4 times because the information that I acquired was much too basic for my mind to equate the strategy into my game plan.

"Read EVERYTHING you can get your hands on! It will only make you a better lawyer."
~ Monique Sexton, Esq.

Another lesson that I learned was to pay whatever monetary fee required for the information. Spend that "bread". Time is money. Failing the bar the first go around also gave me a moment to sit back and take everything in. Now, I see that those potential employers were not the best choice for me and the firm I ended up interning for while studying for the 2nd bar exam was right where I needed to be. Many people pass the bar the first time, but you can't judge your life based upon that standard. I know God had his hand in the mix and I greatly appreciate the lessons that I learned during that period of time.

MAJOR KEY:

You truly learn from your failures. Innately, we don't take account of what makes us win because it's not really important. Heck, we won! Losing makes you take a full account of yourself, your habits, work ethic, and actions.

How to Evaluate Your First Employer

1. Area of Law – Your job should match the desire to practice law in your specialty area.

2. Who is Your Boss? – Do you connect with their vision? Do they just want to get rich off of your hard work? Check their turnover rate, bar complaints, and client concerns. Are they known for being difficult to work with? If you are starting your own firm, start your firm in your hometown where you have a network.

3. Location – Does the location fit your lifestyle? If you are single, get a job in Small Town America. It's easier to learn the law in Small Town America.

4.   Salary – Take less pay if the experience and connections are worth it. Can you still find a way to make ends meet?

5.   The Culture – What clients does the employer typically serve? How many like-minded individuals are employed there?

6.   The Long Game – Don't take the job if you know that you'll be gone in a year. Also, find other minorities that you can learn from.

Law Practice Begins - The Pressure

My situation was unique after passing the bar. A small family-based firm in my local neighborhood employed me. If you wish to remain close to home when becoming a lawyer and are offered this type of an opportunity after passing the bar, consider yourself lucky.

Litigation

I had confidence when trying cases as a brand new lawyer. My training at Regent, primarily through Professor James Duane, gave me the confidence to go straight from law school to the Supreme Court, so I thought. Confidence can mean everything sometimes! I never doubted my training. This is relevant because during the first few weeks of practice, I tried some major cases and it earned the respect of my peers early in my career. I fought as if my life were at stake. I couldn't imagine a young man going to prison on my watch. However, sooner or later, as the great Johnnie Cochran has stated, you will lose. It happens. Every great trial attorney loses but you have to continue to try cases and keep moving forward.

"Don't be afraid to try new things! Trying new things will help you develop your own style of practice!"
~ Monique Sexton, Esq.

As a brand new attorney, you may gain zero respect from your older peers, whether you are Black, White, or Gold. The only way that you'll earn their respect is by trying cases and earning money. Win, lose, or draw...fight like hell! As many great observers have noted, David grabbed his weapon, ran out, and took the battle to Goliath. The more cases you try, the less you will have to try. Once the opposing counsel knows that you can't be bullied, you get better results for your clients.

"Think outside the box."
~ *L. Clifton Smith, III, Esq.*

Clients and Fees

Its factual, dealing with some Black clients (as a Black attorney), you may have to be stern regarding your fees but balance community relationship, as well. This means that you should get all of the names of everyone who will be responsible for this fee in writing, from the jump. You can't do favors or you'll literally end up in the poor house, while spending countless hours away from your family. Once you understand your worth, charge the amount of time and effort you are willing to put into each case. There is nothing wrong with taking a case pro bono. You'll know when the time is right to assist a client free of charge. I've taken cases pro bono for the rich and poor, as well as Black, White, and Hispanic.

Black Lawyers and Black Client Relationships

All great lawyers legitimately care about their clients. As a Black lawyer, your Black clients may expect you to work harder for them and you'll feel the added pressure, especially, if you practice in your hometown. The catch is, some will expect you to work harder but may attempt to slight you on your fee, while being willing to paying your White counterparts double. In other words, some will want every discount or hookup but expect you to do all but lose your license for their case. Be watchful.

Practice Tip:

> *Watch your market and learn how much the average person can afford to pay for your services. If you plan to go into private practice, it's not wise to place your firm in the poorest county in the state. Clients won't be able to afford your services or the market rate and it'll force you out of business.*

> *Don't be a push over on billing.* Don't become known as the attorney who doesn't collect all of his/her fees from his/her clients. This information spreads just as quickly as your reputation does for being a Giant Slayer. Hold your client to his/her contractual obligation until your fee is paid in full. Don't take your foot off the gas.

The Pressure

Thurgood Marshall won major cases with all White male juries in the Jim Crow south. Could you imagine knowing that if you lose your case, your client is going to be murdered immediately, and you as their lawyer, may not make it home whether you win or lose? It's said that the Ku Klux Klan was rallying outside while Marshall was trying his case. He accepted the challenge. In many jurisdictions, judges are elected officials and so are the district attorneys. Some of their decisions, especially, on a large scale, may be political and used to enhance their likelihood of being re-elected and gain favor with the major players.

For example:

On April 12, 2015, Freddie Carlos Gray, Jr., a 25-year old African American man, was arrested by the Baltimore Police Department and died while being transported in the police van. The cause of his death was ascribed to injuries of the spinal cord. Eyewitnesses claimed that the Baltimore police officers used excessive force while arresting Gray.

Six Baltimore police officers were suspended with pay. Following this incident, there was civil unrest in the city of Baltimore. On May 1, 2015, The Baltimore City State's Attorney, Marilyn Mosby, announced that she would be charging the six police officers after the medical examiner ruled Gray's death a homicide. The grand jury indicted the officers on May 21, 2015. There trial against Officer William Porter ended in mistrial, Officers Nero, Goodson, and Rice were found not guilty, and the remaining charges against the other officers were dropped on July 27, 2016.

On September 12, 2017, the U.S. Department of Justice announced that they would not bring federal charges against the six Baltimore police officers that were involved in the arrest of Freddie Gray.

Ever since the Freddie Gray incident, the Baltimore Police Department, as well as, some policy makers, appears to hold resentment towards State's Attorney Mosby and her decision to charge the six police officers involved in the arrest and death of Freddie Gray. Possibly, for these reasons, it may be a little difficult for her to win re-election.

Trial Practice Tip:

Every jury is winnable if you can find the angle of the jury members.

Selecting the Right Clients

If you practice in a small town, you'll get many calls from minorities claiming to be aggrieved. It is your job to take immediate control of the situation and double investigate claims against your potential client. Make sure you do a cost benefit analysis of your time and reputation. Individuals within the community will identify you with your work and the clients you serve. In short, when opposing counsel hears your name, they need to know that you mean business, that you've done your homework, and that you're not being politically forced to fight a losing cause. Remember, your influence is all that you have. If your reputation is at stake, charge triple.

Practice Tip:

> *Keep your mentors on call and always run heavy political cases by them before jumping into something that could tarnish your influence.*

> Keep a referral list in your conference room. Don't be afraid to say no. It'll be hard at first, but practice saying no if you have to. If you don't practice saying no, the hardship of being involved with unwanted cases would be a teacher within its self.

Practice Tip:

> *Never underestimate a case. You must assume that if you represent a political figure (County Commissioner or Mayor, etc.), that you'll be in the newspaper and spotlight. Non-lawyers tend to assume that you agree and align with your client's views, especially, if you are a minority. So make sure that you weigh that cost before*

representing someone that is in the limelight and charge accordingly.

Adverse Cases

We all know you have good cops and bad cops. Most importantly, you have some law enforcement officials that feel a sense of entitlement. Law enforcement officers expect to be given the nod of approval when it is their word versus the word of a criminal defendant, because of the responsibility their job entails. As suggested earlier, Police chiefs and sheriffs have the ability to leverage the district attorney with voter support when they feel the prosecutors are not pushing the cases brought before the court.

This does not only specifically apply to police officers involved as the charging agent of the state. It can be a Department of Social Services agent, probation officer, teacher, principal, or anyone in a position to injure your client. Always remember that these are agents of the state.

Anytime an individual is in opposition to an economical machine, such as the state or a big corporation, there will be underlying issues that weigh against your client.

"Learn the difference between studying and preparing for class. Learn the difference between being a lawyer and running a business."

~ Tyrrell Clemons, Esq.

Bottom Line:

In a criminal case, you are the only person that is going to stand for your client when he has an opposing view of a law enforcement official. The easy call for the judge is to convict your client even if there is reasonable doubt. Law enforcement and some judges may frown upon you if you push too hard as a young attorney against veteran government agents. I personally feel this microscope is intensified if you are a minority attorney, in the south. There are times when I've beat up state's witnesses pretty bad on the stand during cross examination and caught hell for it.

However, if a lawyer has enough stock with the court, it's just business as usual. I'm not saying White lawyers do not catch hell. They do. Quickly, I understand or got the feeling from the court, that it's just not the place of a Black lawyer to put law enforcement officials in "their place" for any malfeasance. I've been called everything but a child of God! I've been called a nigger, and you name it, by officers who felt I shouldn't question their integrity, all because they wore a badge. This is 2018, not the 1960's. Every day you have to balance this fight.

I would like to note that many law enforcement officials located me after a heated trial and congratulated me after a great battle. They are true professionals and recognize the long game. It's the same long game as in law school. No matter how hard you fight, the power is and will stay where it is. With time, I learned the key non-aggressive words to use during trial. It's absolutely vital to learn these key words because if you jump out at law enforcement and your client is found guilty, the judge will punish your client severely.

Example:

Once, during a DWI trial, I questioned the state trooper's motive for asking my client to complete a sobriety test before he checked my client for major injuries after a car wreck. I believe that I suggested the trooper's duty was to protect and then investigate. Thurgood Marshall taught to battle issues more procedurally if possible, rather than, attacking the main or controversial issues in society, and it'll be better for your client. The system is just not built to deal with the heavy issues in an open court forum. As a young lawyer, it seems like blasphemy to choose not to go after your strongest argument but the wise owl fights differently.

Major Key:

You can't say or ask the same things that your counterparts say or ask in court and expect the same treatment when questioning the status quo. If you do, be prepared to fight. If you don't fight, your client and/or the court won't respect you. There's no middle ground, young lion.

Example:

Imagine you are a homebuilder. You are paid to build a home on a certain lot, by a person with major influence within the community, who will bring you more business. However, you'll need to get permission to build the home. Also, you must purchase the materials from a business owner who does not want the lot to be built, nor does he want your client living in the community. You can build the home against the business owner's will, but your relationship with him may be damaged; resulting in the possibility of not being able to purchase materials for future clients from this certain business owner.

Metaphorically, these are the type of situations that one may experience as an attorney. One will be forced to make decisions that could last for years to follow and sometimes the remainder of one's career. Choose wisely.

"Connections. Successful people in this field have a wealth of good contacts for career guidance, emotional support, etc. Good grades are awesome. But making good contacts is much better."

~ Jarrette Pittman, Esq.

A Day In the Life

I want you to peek into the life that I grind in, as a Criminal Defense Attorney. Occasionally, I record audio of my day. It helps me to decompress, gather perspective, and ultimately, close out the day. These are transcribed excerpts from those moments. Depending on the case, some days are tougher than others; in the same token, you get to relish on wins every now and then. I want to always remain transparent and honest to you, my audience.

Service

At the end of the day, it's about the people. You'll learn law on top of law on top of law while in law school, but it's all about the people. The people you serve create income for you. If you remove the people from the equation, there is no service. The people create the situations that create the laws. Laws govern people. You are asking, "What are you saying Finch"? I'm saying, no matter how high or low you go in law practice, you'll still deal with people where they're currently standing in life. One of my clients had a heart attack in the middle of a drug case and court ended for the week. Why? It's because law practice is all about the people. A heart attack is a people problem that trumps the law. Go to the people and embrace them. Learn people and you'll be a better lawyer, you'll attract more clients, and you'll be a happier person. It's all about the people.

Stress

Being a lawyer can be stressful and rewarding. When you think of your position as an advocate, often times, you are standing in the place of the person you are representing and you realize what you say, write, file, and strategize determines whether you add to a person's wins or losses in life. That could mean the difference of hundreds of thousands of dollars, someone's freedom, liberty interests, marriage, child custody, or relationship. Law school allows you to see things in a funnel. You are there, doing case law, but there's no person. You're doing it for a grade, surrounded by high stress. You want to do well in law school, but the consequences of doing poorly are only flunking out. In law practice, people experience a real consequence.

Your workload may determine how well you execute. If you file the wrong motion or impress upon a client to plead guilty/no contest, it may mean a loss of money, jail time, financial ruin, and familial disruption for your client. Paying close attention to the case and its details makes all the difference and can put you on the winning or losing side. Your experience, workload, and how well you manage stress can contribute to the success of your case. Whenever clients and anyone else who is involved with a case call you, they are concerned about their matters; you are concerned about them too. It's always helpful to put yourself in their shoes. However, you must remember that you are the expert in the matter. The client came to you for your expertise in that specific area of law. Don't shy away from your confidence.

Your client is depending on you to deliver. In order to manage stress, you must manage expectations, first. If you're able to manage their expectations well, there's less pressure on you. If you encounter a client who does not have a good case, inform them. If there is a high possibility that the case will not work in your client's favor, let them know upfront or as soon as you came to that realization. Let them know that you will mitigate the case on their behalf to the best of your ability.

46

Explain the possible outcomes of their case so that the client and their families may be prepared for the worst-case scenarios. Open, honest dialogue between yourself and the client will ease some of the stress and pressure for you.

If it's a big win or a big loss, the introduction of a jury or judge making the final decision can cause a lot of sleepless nights and you may find yourself working through the night. Just discussing the case with your client who appears to be broken by the whole ordeal, can trigger a visceral reaction. For example, if someone is convicted of a DWI, he/she could lose his or her job, driver's license, etc. A client's child may have received a charge that could possibly mar their educational record. Situations such as these, can weigh heavily on you if you're not able to balance the stress well. As an attorney, you take on the emotion of the individual of which you are advocating for. If there's a lot of work to do, it will pull from you emotionally. If you know that it's an easy fix, it can drastically reduce your stress load. Your family, kids, wife, husband, bills, etc...everyone needs you operating at 100% at work, as well as, at home.

If you are not married, managing your stress is slightly easier, because only your work is dependent upon you. This is a cakewalk in either dynamic. You must do what works for you. Everyone's life and lifestyle is different. However, you don't want your house to fall apart, so you must maintain it with time, care, love, and attention. You can't concentrate on the stress. You should only concentrate on the work. Clients only want results, not excuses. If you are considering becoming a lawyer, managing people and emotions is a pertinent component of the work. If these areas were not your strong suit, I would advise you to seek another career in law that doesn't manage people and emotions as much.

In my conversations with corporate lawyers, they often reference their lack of human interaction. Corporate lawyers are managing businesses, not people. They almost never build personal relationships with their clients. I try to give myself one day a week to reflect, pray, clear my mind, do personal development tasks, meditate, and simply relax. You might have to take a day or two after a big trial and sleep in for 2-3 days to reboot your mind. Consequently, it is important to be in tune with yourself and your personal needs on a soul level or you could easily burn yourself out.

Major Point:

> *When you put on the lawyer hat, you must be able to manage stress. Before you consider law school, if you have any vices, i.e. drugs, alcohol, etc., the vices will only become more magnified as you encounter the stressful environments of lawyering.*

I suggest that you try to cut those vices off and become as spiritually independent of them as possible. For example, if you are not a good steward with your time and money, your law firm will struggle financially or not maximize its profit. The key is to work as hard as you can while developing an economic mindset. It would be best to hire people who can alleviate stress from you. If you're a trial lawyer, you need to concentrate on trial and trial prep. You will lose some cases. You need to be able to deal with the stress of alerting your client of the pros/cons. Never make promises that you cannot guarantee. Always give your client options. I repeatedly provide my clients with my insight to keep them abreast and aware of everything. If you're not sure, you need to let the client know what your strategy is.

If you are married, you need to do some soul searching with your mate to stay on the same page as the spouse. They need to know your workload, travel schedule, etc. Being a lawyer is very rewarding. It's a life's work. If you work it part time, you'll only make the part-time money. If you approach it half-heartedly, your work will not be as satisfying.

"Change your major. Get your MBA."
~ Jamal Summey, Esq.

The Lying Client

Often times, a client will sit down across from you at the conference room table and tell you lies. Generally, I expect my clients not to be 100% truthful with me because most people aren't the first time you meet with them. After building a little bit of a rapport, my clients will be 95 to 100 percent truthful about what transpired in their case. It is difficult to properly advocate for my client or to be their last line of defense when I don't have all of the facts. I do have a certain advantage where the state has to present a burden of proof. As the defendant, I don't have to prove anything. If the evidence presented against my client is dramatically different, I will determine if the client is lying. Consequently, I will share the inconsistencies with them and try to show them that it's not believable to a jury. If the jury does not believe his lie, he won't win. I never tell the person outright that he/she is lying. Either way, I will still fight for them and I can sleep at night. Your lawyer can only help you as much as you are honest about the situation. If there is a guilty verdict, he needs to know that you were only able to assist them with the amount of foresight and knowledge the client provided you with in order to represent them in court. Whenever a criminal defendant goes inside of a courtroom, the jury, judge, and law enforcement already have preconceived notions about the defendant. As their advocate, it's your job to give them a fair chance of representing themselves in the best light possible.

A Loss

How does it feel to lose a case? How does it feel to go in front of a judge and lose a case? What did your client actually lose? There have been several times where I've tried a case and there is a preliminary hearing, and I needed evidence for the record of which I could use for final trial but was unable to secure it. Is it really a lose? If my client and I go to war and he has some good issues or is innocent and we lose, it hurts like hell! It really does...especially when there is no recourse. I might lose some sleep over it.

There will be times that you'll suggest to the client that it's not in their best interest to try a case and they ignore you. It hurts you. They might go to jail, prison or have to pay large amounts of money. If the judge or jury comes back and decides that they have to do time, I won't lose sleep. I always advise: Listen to your lawyer. And if you can't listen to your lawyer, find one that you *can* listen to.

Molly Guy

I just finished a trial with a guy who was charged with multiple counts of drug possession with the intent to sell...molly. Just to recap, eventually, he was sentenced to 26 months in prison. In the beginning of the week, I told him that he could go home on probation. He wanted to fight the charge. The evidence was clear. He was on video unscrewing a DVD player with a substance that appeared to be molly and gave it to a confidential informant. The confidential informant testified in court. This confidential informant was a paid informant and was not working off his charges...making him a little but more reliable. He only wanted to see if he could beat the system and off principle. If you hire a lawyer, you have to trust them.

Trust your lawyer. The court does not care about your feelings or personal interest. Please make sure that you don't jeopardize your freedom. It's your life vs. your life. I let my client know that he could have easily gone home on probation. Every night, he only revved himself up for trial. My job was not to tell him what he wanted to hear. My job was to present him with the best options available to him. At the end, I fought it to the best of my ability and still lost. When in doubt, trust your lawyer.

Networking and Time Management

Ultimately, becoming a successful attorney is less about your trial skills and more about your network of influence, and the amount of territory your good name covers. As great of a trial lawyer Johnnie Cochran was before O.J. Simpson, he didn't have the influence to call in favors on the east coast until he was a household name.

Most lawyers have an average amount of influence outside of their specialty areas to get hired for cases. However, to get the case, you must have a network of people who trust you and the distance of your influence and reputation must be substantial enough to reach that pool of clients. Therefore, you must aim to become the most dynamic influencer possible.

Moreover, a lawyer makes money by saving time, not by working hard, countless hours.

Example:

Brenda works 14 hours on a Worker's Compensation issue to make $2500.00. Brenda calls her friend Sarah, a Worker's Compensation attorney. Sarah works 2 hours on the issue and Sarah and Brenda split $2500.00. While Sarah is working on the Worker's Compensation issue, Brenda has 11.5 hours of free time to work on her current Family Law caseload where she billed $3500.00 for working 11.5 hours.

Surely, Brenda would've made more money by doing the work herself and not having Sarah help her with the case. However, by allowing Sarah to help with the case, she was able to clear free hours to bill on her current caseload. The key is that Brenda had the network or influence to call in help, save time, maximize the dollar, and strengthen her relationship with Sarah. Who do you think Sarah will call when she has a Family Law referral? Of course, she will call Brenda.

You Got Next

Life is like a game of pickup basketball. You practice at the house or with your boys at the local gym, just trying to get your skills up. And then one day, you go to the big court. Nobody recognizes you. Or, maybe they do?

For all of those that don't know how pickup ball works: You pick five people. You play, win or lose. If you lose, you get off the court. The way you get a game is by saying, "I GOT NEXT".

There may be six, eight...even twelve men waiting ahead of you, but you won't play until you call next. So, the first time you go to the court, it dawns on you that you're not 7'10, 6'8 or even a meager 6'3. It's a known fact that a regular guard that is 5'9 and 180 lbs. are a dime a dozen. So what are you going to do? Wait? Hope for the next man to pick you up? Or are you going to call next? Are you going to have the courage to call next? Get your squad and go out and compete! I tell you...success is all about having the courage to call next! Pick your team and go out there and dominate!

So what?! You didn't get into that college or that Ivy League school. Neither did you get into that top elite law school. You didn't pass the bar on the first try. An elite law firm overlooked you in 2nd round interviews. Are you going to wait on the system or are you going to break the system? So, go ahead...CALL NEXT! Build your squad, build your team, and dominate. Don't let this world system dictate your next move.

"Use your voice, your knowledge, and skill set on behalf of the vulnerable and marginalized people whether in criminal, family, child welfare, juvenile, immigration court, etc. When you are living in your dream neighborhood and all is good for you and your family, recall that there are cousins, siblings, etc. who remain in a struggle to not just thrive, but they struggle to exist in the current political and social climate. We, who have been given much, are required to contribute much. We must strive not just for success, but significance. Therefore, do all in your power to develop your skill, your voice, and your confidence...as there are millions waiting for whom you may be their only voice.
~Watsi Sutton, Esq.

About the Author

My name is Johnnie Finch. I am a North Carolina criminal defense attorney. I represent people who have been charge with criminal offenses, such as, driving while impaired, probation violations, and drug offenses.

I went to law school because I enjoy advocating for others. My first experience with the criminal justice system came from watching the famous criminal defense attorney, Johnnie Cochran, match wits with Marcia Clark during the O.J. Simpson trial. His confidence, knowledge of the law, and charisma were inspiring! Flash forward 17 years, and I've traded my Nike Airs for some hard-bottom lace-ups and a briefcase.

After college, I had the opportunity to counsel teens that had been charged with both, juvenile and adult criminal offenses. Working for the NC Department of Juvenile Justice for seven years, I realized my passion for working with everyday people with real problems, such as, being fired from a job, having their driver's license revoked, or being a victim of high school bullying. I chose to fight in this arena opposed to handling big corporation issues.

After being admitted into the North Carolina Bar in 2013, I have practiced in the area of criminal defense, exclusively. During this time, I've effectively handled hundreds of traffic and criminal law matters by taking an assertive approach. My strategy is simple. We get results by taking a stand for our client's issues despite the interests of the state. Zealous representation. Since opening The Law Office of Johnnie L. Finch, Jr., PLLC, in January of 2016, we have expanded our practice to handle Automotive Injury, Catastrophic Injury, and

Wrongful Death matters, just as my hero, Attorney Cochran had ventured.

My practice area extends primarily throughout NC's District 1 (Perquimans, Pasquotank, Dare, Gates, Chowan, Currituck, and Camden Counties) and surrounding counties (Tyrrell, Hertford, and Bertie).

On a personal note, I married the love of my life, Meron, April 11, 2015. We met on the campus of Regent University while she was earning her M. Div. in Theology and a Masters in Counseling. She is incredible and I love her to life! Our son, Johnnie III, also known as "John John", was born on March 8, 2016 and our daughter, Yohanna, was born on July 10, 2017.

I embrace all opportunities to give encouraging talks with youths and adults covering various topics, such as, cyber bullying, crimes related to social networking, and law school advice. My most recent speaking engagement was with the Elizabeth City State University Criminal Justice Club with the topic being, "Surviving Life After the Big Walk Across the Stage". I look forward to participating in future speaking engagements and reaching as many individuals as possible.